ice cream

ice cream

Love Food ® is an imprint of Parragon Books Ltd

Parragon
Queen Street House
4 Queen Street
Bath BA1 1HE, UK

Cover design by Talking Design
Written by Susanna Tee
Photography by Clive Streeter
Home economy by Angela Drake

ISBN 978-1-4075-6275-9

Printed in China

Notes for the reader
• This book uses both metric and imperial measurements. Follow the same units of measurement throughout; do not mix metric and imperial. All spoon measurements are level: teaspoons are assumed to be 5 ml, and tablespoons are assumed to be 15 ml. Unless otherwise stated, milk is assumed to be full fat, eggs and individual vegetables are medium, and pepper is freshly ground black pepper.
• The times given are an approximate guide only. Preparation times differ according to the techniques used by different people and the cooking times may also vary from those given. Optional ingredients, variations or serving suggestions have not been included in the calculations.
• Recipes using raw or very lightly cooked eggs should be avoided by infants, the elderly, pregnant women, convalescents and anyone suffering from an illness. Pregnant and breastfeeding women are advised to avoid eating peanuts and peanut products. Sufferers from nut allergies should be aware that some of the ready-made ingredients used in the recipes in this book may contain nuts. Always check the packaging before use.

Contents

Ice Cream

Ice Creams

Ice cream is the number one treat to eat on its own or to boost another dessert. It is definitely a favourite with children and making home-made ice creams is simple – you will all enjoy the fun of freezing! Another plus point is that it is good to know exactly what ingredients have been used in the process. However luxurious and indulgent ice cream may be, there is no substitute for the home-made variety whether flavoured with pure vanilla, packed with dark chocolate, soft summer berries, chopped nuts, coffee or caramel toffee.

Making at Home

The important part of making ice cream is to churn the mixture during the freezing process to break up the ice crystals and produce a smooth, creamy texture. The exception is ice cream made with yogurt as over-beating can cause the yogurt to separate. An ice cream machine isn't essential but it does save time and eliminates the need for you to keep beating the mixture. It is well worth investing in a machine and they come in different shapes, sizes and types, along with different price tags! A basic ice cream machine will churn the mixture in a pre-frozen container while more expensive countertop machines will also freeze the mixture in their own freezer units.

The Essential Ingredients

The basic ingredients in most ice cream recipes are full-fat milk, caster sugar, egg yolks, cream and natural flavourings. If you want to save time and the recipe uses an egg custard base, then a carton of fresh custard could be used as an alternative. The recipes also often use whipping cream. If you find this difficult to buy, then you can use half double and half single cream.

Ten Top Tips for Delicious Ice Cream

• It helps to chill the ingredients before starting as this speeds up the freezing process.

• The recipes require you, if freezing in a freezer, to beat the ice cream once during freezing. If you have time, a second beating would be beneficial to create a smooth ice cream.

• When making fruit ice creams choose the freshest, ripest fruit and avoid using any blemished fruit.

• Don't be tempted to make too large a quantity of ice cream unless you are going to serve it all at once, as the continual removing of a few scoops at a time will quickly cause ice crystals to form and lead to deterioration.

• Fill the container in which you are freezing the ice cream to within 1 cm/½ inch of the top and, once the ice cream reaches that level, lay a piece of non-stick baking paper on top to prevent ice crystals forming on the surface.

• Home-made ice creams are best if stored for no longer than two months because, without stabilizers or preservatives usually found in commercial ice creams, their flavour, colour and texture will deteriorate.

• To make serving easier, remove from the freezer and leave at room temperature for 15–30 minutes to soften, or temper, slightly. Alternatively, soften in the microwave, on HIGH, in bursts of 30 seconds. Do not allow the ice cream to melt before returning to the freezer.

• Keep a selection of crisp, thin biscuits in the store cupboard to accompany ice cream. Cones are also useful for serving scoops to children.

• With the leftover egg whites, make a batch of crisp, tiny meringues to serve with the ice cream.

• For an attractive finish, serve fruit ice creams with a little of the fresh fruit from which it was made, for example a scattering of blueberries on Blueberry Ice Cream and raspberries on Raspberry Ripple Ice Cream.

The Classics

serves 4–6

600 ml/1 pint whipping cream or 300 ml/10 fl oz double cream and 300 ml/ 10 fl oz single cream

1 vanilla pod

4 large egg yolks

115 g/4 oz caster sugar

rich vanilla ice cream

Pour the whipping cream into a large heavy-based saucepan. Split open the vanilla pod and scrape out the seeds into the cream, then add the whole vanilla pod, too. Bring almost to the boil, then remove from the heat and leave to infuse for 30 minutes.

Put the egg yolks and sugar in a large bowl and whisk together until pale and the mixture leaves a trail when the whisk is lifted. Remove the vanilla pod from the cream, then slowly add the cream to the egg mixture, stirring all the time with a wooden spoon. Strain the mixture into the rinsed-out saucepan or a double boiler and cook over a low heat for 10–15 minutes, stirring all the time, until the mixture thickens enough to coat the back of the spoon. Do not allow the mixture to boil or it will curdle. Remove the custard from the heat and leave to cool for at least 1 hour, stirring from time to time to prevent a skin from forming.

If using an ice cream machine, churn the cold custard in the machine following the manufacturer's instructions. Alternatively, freeze the custard in a freezerproof container, uncovered, for 1–2 hours, or until it begins to set around the edges. Turn the custard into a bowl and stir with a fork or beat in a food processor until smooth. Return to the freezer and freeze.

serves 4–6

300 ml/10 fl oz milk

1 vanilla pod

100 g/3½ oz plain chocolate

3 egg yolks

85 g/3 oz caster sugar

300 ml/10 fl oz double cream

chocolate ice cream

Pour the milk into a large heavy-based saucepan, split open the vanilla pod and scrape out the seeds into the milk and then add the whole vanilla pod, too. Bring almost to the boil then remove from the heat and leave to infuse for 30 minutes. Remove the vanilla pod from the milk. Break the chocolate into the milk and heat gently, stirring all the time, until melted and smooth.

Put the egg yolks and sugar in a large bowl and whisk together until pale and the mixture leaves a trail when the whisk is lifted. Slowly add the chocolate mixture, stirring all the time with a wooden spoon. Strain the mixture into the rinsed-out saucepan or a double boiler and cook over a low heat for 10–15 minutes, stirring all the time, until the mixture thickens enough to coat the back of a wooden spoon. Do not allow the mixture to boil or it will curdle. Remove the custard from the heat and leave to cool for at least 1 hour, stirring from time to time to prevent a skin from forming. Meanwhile, whip the cream until it holds its shape. Keep in the refrigerator until ready to use.

If using an ice cream machine, fold the whipped cream into the cold custard, then churn the mixture in the machine following the manufacturer's instructions. Alternatively, freeze the custard in a freezerproof container, uncovered, for 1–2 hours, or until it begins to set around the edges. Turn the custard into a bowl and stir with a fork or beat in a food processor until smooth. Fold in the whipped cream. Return to the freezer and freeze for a further 2–3 hours, or until firm or required. Cover the container with a lid for storing.

serves 6

85 g/3 oz raisins

3 tbsp rum

600 ml/1 pint whipping cream

1 vanilla pod

4 large egg yolks

115 g/4 oz caster sugar

rum & raisin ice cream

Put the raisins in a bowl, add the rum and stir together. Leave to soak for 2–3 hours, stirring occasionally, until the liquid is absorbed. Meanwhile, pour the cream into a heavy-based saucepan. Split open the vanilla pod and scrape out the seeds into the cream, then add the whole vanilla pod, too. Bring almost to the boil, then remove from the heat and leave to infuse for 30 minutes. Put the egg yolks and sugar in a large bowl and whisk together until pale and the mixture leaves a trail when the whisk is lifted. Remove the vanilla pod from the cream, then slowly add the cream to the egg mixture, stirring all the time with a wooden spoon.

Strain the mixture into the rinsed-out saucepan or a double boiler and cook over a low heat for 10–15 minutes, stirring all the time, until the mixture thickens enough to coat the back of the wooden spoon. Do not allow the mixture to boil or it will curdle. Remove the custard from the heat and leave to cool for at least 1 hour, stirring from time to time to prevent a skin from forming.

If using an ice cream machine, churn the cold custard in the machine following the manufacturer's instructions. Just before the ice cream freezes, add the soaked raisins. Alternatively, freeze the custard in a freezerproof container, uncovered, for 1–2 hours, or until it begins to set around the edges. Turn the custard into a bowl and stir with a fork or beat in a food processor until smooth. Fold in the soaked raisins. Return to the freezer and freeze for a further 2–3 hours, or until firm or required. Cover the container with a lid for storing.

serves 6

300 ml/10 fl oz milk

3 egg yolks

85 g/3 oz light soft
brown sugar

450-g/1-lb jar Dulce de Leche
(caramel toffee)

300 ml/10 fl oz whipping
cream

toffee ice cream

Pour the milk into a heavy-based saucepan and bring almost to the boil. Remove from the heat. Put the egg yolks and sugar in a large bowl and whisk together until pale and the mixture leaves a trail when the whisk is lifted. Slowly add the milk, stirring all the time with a wooden spoon.

Strain the mixture into the rinsed-out saucepan or a double boiler and cook over a low heat for 10–15 minutes, stirring all the time, until the mixture thickens enough to coat the back of the wooden spoon. Do not allow the mixture to boil or it will curdle.

Remove the custard from the heat, add the caramel toffee and whisk together until smooth. Leave to cool for at least 1 hour, stirring from time to time to prevent a skin from forming. Meanwhile, whip the cream until it holds its shape. Keep in the refrigerator until ready to use.

If using an ice cream machine, fold the whipped cream into the cold custard, then churn the mixture in the machine following the manufacturer's instructions. Alternatively, freeze the custard in a freezerproof container, uncovered, for 1–2 hours, or until it begins to set around the edges. Turn the custard into a bowl and stir with a fork or beat in a food processor until smooth. Fold in the whipped cream. Return to the freezer and freeze for a further 2–3 hours, or until firm or required. Cover the container with a lid for storing.

serves 6

300 ml/10 fl oz single cream

1/2 tsp peppermint extract

4 egg yolks

115 g/4 oz caster sugar

200 g/7 oz plain chocolate
peppermint crisps

300 ml/10 fl oz double cream

mint choc chip ice cream

Pour the cream into a heavy-based saucepan and bring almost to the boil. Remove from the heat and stir in the peppermint extract. Put the egg yolks and sugar in a large bowl and whisk together until pale and the mixture leaves a trail when the whisk is lifted. Slowly add the warm cream, stirring all the time with a wooden spoon.

Strain the mixture into the rinsed-out saucepan or a double boiler and cook over a low heat for 10–15 minutes, stirring all the time, until the mixture thickens enough to coat the back of the wooden spoon. Do not allow the mixture to boil or it will curdle. Remove the custard from the heat and leave to cool for at least 1 hour, stirring from time to time to prevent a skin from forming. Meanwhile, put the peppermint crisps, a few at a time, into a food processor and chop into small pieces. Alternatively, chop the peppermint crisps into small pieces by hand. Whip the double cream until it holds its shape. Keep in the refrigerator until ready to use.

If using an ice cream machine, fold the whipped cream into the cold custard, then churn the mixture in the machine following the manufacturer's instructions. Just before the ice cream freezes, add the peppermint crisp pieces. Alternatively, freeze the custard in a freezerproof container, uncovered, for 1–2 hours, or until it begins to set around the edges. Turn the custard into a bowl and stir with a fork or beat in a food processor until smooth. Fold in the whipped cream and peppermint crisp pieces. Return to the freezer and freeze for a further 2–3 hours, or until firm or required. Cover the container with a lid for storing.

serves 6

300 ml/10 fl oz milk

85 g/3 oz soft dark brown sugar

55 g/2 oz butter

2 eggs

70 g/2$\frac{1}{2}$ oz caster sugar

1 tsp vanilla extract

300 ml/10 fl oz whipping cream

100 g/3$\frac{1}{2}$ oz pecan nuts, finely chopped

butterscotch & pecan ice cream

Pour the milk into a saucepan and bring almost to the boil. Remove from the heat. Melt the butter in a heavy-based saucepan, stir in the brown sugar and heat gently until the sugar melts, then boil for 1 minute, or until beginning to caramelize, being careful not to allow the mixture to burn. Remove from the heat and slowly stir in the milk. Return to the heat and heat gently, stirring all the time, until well blended. Remove from the heat and leave to cool slightly. Put the eggs and caster sugar in a large bowl and whisk together until pale. Slowly add the warm milk and vanilla extract, stirring all the time with a wooden spoon.

Strain the mixture into the rinsed-out saucepan or a double boiler and cook over a low heat for 10–15 minutes, stirring all the time, until the mixture thickens enough to coat the back of the wooden spoon. Do not allow the mixture to boil or it will curdle. Remove the custard from the heat and leave to cool for at least 1 hour, stirring from time to time to prevent a skin from forming. Meanwhile, whip the cream until it holds its shape. Keep in the refrigerator until ready to use.

If using an ice cream machine, fold the whipped cream into the cold custard, then churn the mixture in the machine following the manufacturer's instructions. Just before the ice cream freezes, add the chopped pecan nuts. Alternatively, freeze the custard in a freezerproof container, uncovered, for 1–2 hours, or until it begins to set around the edges. Turn the custard into a bowl and stir with a fork or beat in a food processor until smooth. Fold in the whipped cream and chopped pecan nuts. Return to the freezer and freeze for a further 2–3 hours, or until firm or required. Cover the container with a lid for storing.

serves 6–8

85 g/3 oz granulated sugar

2 tbsp golden syrup

1 tsp bicarbonate of soda

400 ml/14 fl oz whipping cream

1 can condensed milk

honeycomb ice cream

Grease a baking tray. Put the sugar and syrup in a heavy-based saucepan and heat gently until the sugar melts, then boil for 1–2 minutes, or until beginning to caramelize, being careful not to allow the mixture to burn. Stir in the bicarbonate of soda, then immediately pour the mixture onto the prepared baking tray but do not spread. Leave for about 10 minutes until cold.

When the honeycomb is cold, put in a strong polythene bag and crush into small pieces, using a rolling pin or meat mallet. Whip the cream until it holds its shape, then whisk in the condensed milk.

If using an ice cream machine, churn the mixture in the machine following the manufacturer's instructions. Just before the ice cream freezes, add the honeycomb pieces. Alternatively, freeze the custard in a freezerproof container, uncovered, for 1–2 hours, or until it begins to set around the edges. Turn the custard into a bowl and stir with a fork or beat in a food processor until smooth. Fold in the honeycomb pieces. Return to the freezer and freeze for a further 2–3 hours, or until firm or required. Cover the container with a lid for storing.

serves 6

225 g/8 oz caster sugar

150 ml/5 fl oz water

900 g/2 lb fresh strawberries,
plus extra to decorate

juice of 1/2 lemon

juice of 1/2 orange

300ml/10 fl oz whipping
cream

dairy strawberry ice cream

Put the sugar and water in a heavy-based saucepan and heat gently, stirring, until the sugar has dissolved. Bring to the boil, then, without stirring, boil for 5 minutes to form a syrup. Towards the end of the cooking time, keep an eye on the mixture to ensure that it does not burn. Immediately remove the syrup from the heat and leave to cool for at least 1 hour.

Meanwhile, push the strawberries through a nylon sieve into a bowl to form a purée. When the syrup is cold, add the strawberry purée with the lemon juice and orange juice and stir well together. Whip the cream until it holds its shape. Keep in the refrigerator until ready to use.

If using an ice cream machine, fold the strawberry mixture into the whipped cream, then churn in the machine following the manufacturer's instructions. Alternatively, freeze the mixture in a freezerproof container, uncovered, for 1–2 hours, or until it begins to set around the edges. Turn the mixture into a bowl and stir with a fork or beat in a food processor until smooth. Fold in the whipped cream. Return to the freezer and freeze for a further 2–3 hours, or until firm or required. Cover the container with a lid for storing. Serve decorated with strawberries.

serves 6–8

425 ml/15 fl oz milk

1 vanilla pod

6 egg yolks

125 g/4 1/2 oz caster sugar

italian vanilla gelato

Pour the milk into a large heavy-based saucepan, split open the vanilla pod and scrape out the seeds into the milk, then add the whole vanilla pod, too. Bring almost to the boil then remove from the heat and leave to infuse for 30 minutes. Remove the vanilla pod from the milk.

Put the egg yolks and sugar in a large bowl and whisk together until pale and the mixture leaves a trail when the whisk is lifted. Slowly add the milk, stirring all the time with a wooden spoon.

Strain the mixture into the rinsed-out pan or a double boiler and cook over a low heat for 10–15 minutes, stirring all the time, until the mixture thickens slightly. Do not allow the mixture to boil or it will curdle. Remove the custard from the heat and leave to cool for at least 1 hour, stirring from time to time to prevent a skin from forming.

If using an ice cream machine, churn the mixture in the machine following the manufacturer's instructions. Alternatively, freeze the custard in a freezerproof container, uncovered, for 1–2 hours, or until it begins to set around the edges. Turn the custard into a bowl and stir with a fork or beat in a food processor until smooth. Return to the freezer and repeat the breaking up of the ice crystals every 30 minutes for 2 hours. Return to the freezer until firm or required. Cover the container with a lid for storing.

italian pistachio gelato

serves 6–8

850 ml/1¹/2 pints milk

1 vanilla pod

9 egg yolks

175 g/6 oz caster sugar

2 tbsp almond-flavoured liqueur (optional)

few drops of green food colouring (optional)

100 g/3¹/2 oz shelled pistachio nuts

Pour the milk into a heavy-based saucepan, add the vanilla pod and bring almost to the boil. Remove from the heat and leave to infuse for 15 minutes.

Put the egg yolks and sugar in a large bowl and whisk together until pale and the mixture leaves a trail when the whisk is lifted. Remove the vanilla pod from the milk, then slowly add the milk to the egg mixture, stirring all the time with a wooden spoon. Strain the mixture into the rinsed-out saucepan or a double boiler and cook over a low heat for 10–15 minutes, stirring all the time, until the mixture thickens enough to coat the back of the spoon. Do not allow the mixture to boil or it will curdle.

Remove the custard from the heat and leave to cool for at least 1 hour, stirring from time to time to prevent a skin from forming. When the custard is cold, stir in the liqueur, if using, and, if wished, add the food colouring to tint the mixture pale green. Finely chop the nuts.

If using an ice cream machine, churn the cold custard in the machine following the manufacturer's instructions. Just before the ice cream freezes, add the chopped nuts. Alternatively, freeze the custard in a freezerproof container, uncovered, for 1–2 hours, or until it begins to set around the edges. Turn the custard into a bowl and stir with a fork or beat in a food processor until smooth. Return to the freezer and repeat the breaking up of the ice crystals every 30 minutes for 2 hours. Return to the freezer until firm or required. Cover the container with a lid for storing.

Pure
Indulgence

serves *4–6*

300 ml/10 fl oz milk

1 vanilla pod

115 g/4 oz milk chocolate

85 g/3 oz caster sugar

3 egg yolks

300 ml/10 fl oz whipping cream

chocolate chip ice cream

Pour the milk into a heavy-based saucepan, add the vanilla pod and bring almost to the boil. Remove from the heat and leave to infuse for 30 minutes. Meanwhile, chop the chocolate into small pieces and set aside.

Put the sugar and egg yolks in a large bowl and whisk together until pale and the mixture leaves a trail when the whisk is lifted. Remove the vanilla pod from the milk, then slowly add the milk to the sugar mixture, stirring all the time with a wooden spoon. Strain the mixture into the rinsed-out saucepan or a double boiler and cook over a low heat for 10–15 minutes, stirring all the time, until the mixture thickens enough to coat the back of the wooden spoon. Do not allow the mixture to boil or it will curdle. Remove the custard from the heat, cover and leave to cool for at least 1 hour, stirring from time to time to prevent a skin from forming. Meanwhile, whip the cream until it holds its shape. Keep in the refrigerator until ready to use.

If using an ice cream machine, fold the whipped cream into the cold custard, then churn the mixture in the machine following the manufacturer's instructions. Just before the ice cream freezes, add the chocolate pieces. Alternatively, freeze the custard in a freezerproof container, uncovered, for 1–2 hours until beginning to set around the edges. Turn the custard into a bowl and stir with a fork or beat in a food processor until smooth. Fold in the whipped cream and chocolate pieces. Return to the freezer and freeze for a further 2–3 hours, or until firm or required. Cover the container with a lid for storing.

serves 4–6

85 g/3 oz plain dark
chocolate, broken into pieces

300 ml/10 fl oz milk

85 g/3 oz caster sugar

3 egg yolks

300 ml/10 fl oz whipping
cream

praline

vegetable oil, for oiling

100 g/3$\frac{1}{2}$ oz granulated
sugar

2 tbsp water

50 g/1$\frac{3}{4}$ oz blanched
almonds

chocolate praline ice cream

To prepare the praline, brush a baking tray with oil. Put the sugar, water and nuts in a large heavy-based saucepan and heat gently, stirring, until the sugar has dissolved, then let the mixture bubble gently without stirring for 6–10 minutes, or until lightly golden brown. As soon as the mixture has turned golden brown, immediately pour it onto the prepared baking tray and spread it out evenly. Leave to cool for 1 hour, or until cold and hardened. Finely crush the praline in a food processor.

To prepare the ice cream, put the chocolate and milk in a saucepan and heat gently, stirring, until the chocolate has melted and the mixture is smooth. Remove from the heat. Put the sugar and egg yolks in a large bowl and whisk together until pale and the mixture leaves a trail when the whisk is lifted. Slowly add the milk mixture, stirring all the time with a wooden spoon. Strain the mixture into the rinsed-out saucepan or a double boiler and cook over a low heat for 10–15 minutes, stirring all the time, until the mixture thickens enough to coat the back of the spoon. Do not allow the mixture to boil or it will curdle.

Remove the custard from the heat and leave to cool for at least 1 hour, stirring from time to time to prevent a skin from forming. Meanwhile, whip the cream until it holds its shape. Keep in the refrigerator until ready to use.

If using an ice cream machine, fold the cold custard into the whipped cream, then churn the mixture in the machine following the manufacturer's instructions. Just before the ice cream freezes, add the praline. Return to the freezer and freeze for a further 2–3 hours, or until firm or required. Cover the container with a lid for storing.

serves 4–6

300 ml/10 fl oz milk

100 g/4 oz plain chocolate

25 g/1 oz butter

1 tsp vanilla extract

125 g/4$\frac{1}{2}$ oz caster sugar

75 g/2$\frac{3}{4}$ oz golden syrup

4 eggs

300 ml/10 fl oz whipping cream

chocolate fudge ice cream

Pour 175 ml/6 fl oz of the milk into a heavy-based saucepan. Break the chocolate into the milk, add the butter and vanilla extract and heat gently, stirring all the time, until melted and smooth. Stir in the sugar and syrup and heat until the mixture boils. Reduce the heat and simmer for 4 minutes, without stirring. Remove from the heat and leave to cool slightly.

Put the eggs in a bowl and beat together. Slowly add the chocolate mixture, stirring all the time with a wooden spoon.

Strain the mixture into the rinsed-out saucepan or a double boiler and cook over a low heat for 10–15 minutes, stirring all the time, until the mixture thickens enough to coat the back of the wooden spoon. Do not allow the mixture to boil or it will curdle. Remove the custard from the heat and stir in the remaining milk and the cream. Leave to cool for at least 1 hour, stirring from time to time to prevent a skin from forming.

If using an ice cream machine, churn the mixture in the machine following the manufacturer's instructions. Alternatively, freeze the custard in a freezerproof container, uncovered, for 1–2 hours until beginning to set around the edges. Turn the custard into a bowl and stir with a fork or beat in a food processor until smooth. Return to the freezer and freeze for a further 2–3 hours, or until firm or required. Cover the container with a lid for storing.

serves 4–6

300 ml/10 fl oz milk

1/4 tsp vanilla extract

3 egg yolks

85 g/3 oz caster sugar

300 ml/10 fl oz whipping cream

100 g/31/2 oz chocolate flavour sandwich biscuits

chocolate cookie ice cream

Pour the milk into a heavy-based saucepan, add the vanilla extract and bring almost to the boil. Remove from the heat. Put the egg yolks and sugar in a large bowl and whisk together until pale and the mixture leaves a trail when the whisk is lifted. Slowly add the milk to the egg mixture, stirring all the time with a wooden spoon.

Strain the mixture into the rinsed-out saucepan or a double boiler and cook over a low heat for 10–15 minutes, stirring all the time, until the mixture thickens enough to coat the back of the wooden spoon. Do not allow the mixture to boil or it will curdle. Remove the custard from the heat and leave to cool for at lest 1 hour, stirring from time to time to prevent a skin from forming.

Meanwhile, whip the cream until it holds its shape. Keep in the refrigerator until ready to use. Put the biscuits in a strong polythene bag and roughly crush with a rolling pin.

If using an ice cream machine, fold the whipped cream into the cold custard, then churn the mixture in the machine following the manufacturer's instructions. Just before the ice cream freezes, add the crushed biscuits. Alternatively, freeze the custard in a freezerproof container, uncovered, for 1–2 hours until beginning to set around the edges. Turn the custard into a bowl and stir with a fork or beat in a food processor until smooth. Fold in the whipped cream and crushed biscuits. Return to the freezer and freeze for a further 2–3 hours, or until firm or required. Cover the container with a lid for storing.

serves 6

100 g/3¹/₂ oz walnut pieces

150 ml/5 fl oz maple syrup

300 ml/10 fl oz double cream

200 ml/7 fl oz canned
evaporated milk, well chilled

maple syrup &
walnut ice cream

Put the walnut pieces in a food processor and process until
finely chopped, but be careful not to process them into
a purée. Set aside.

Mix the syrup and cream together until well blended. Pour the
chilled evaporated milk into a large bowl and whisk until thick
and doubled in volume. The mixture should leave a trail when
the whisk is lifted. Add the syrup mixture to the whisked milk
and fold together.

If using an ice cream machine, churn the mixture in the
machine following the manufacturer's instructions. Just before
the ice cream freezes, add the chopped nuts. Alternatively,
freeze the mixture in a freezerproof container, uncovered,
for 1–2 hours, or until it begins to set around the edges. Turn
the mixture into a bowl and stir with a fork or beat in a food
processor until smooth. Stir in the chopped nuts, then return to
the freezer and freeze for a further 2–3 hours, or until firm or
required. Cover the container with a lid for storing.

peanut butter ice cream

serves 6–8

300 ml/10 fl oz milk

1 tsp vanilla extract

3 egg yolks

115 g/4 oz caster sugar

425 ml/15 fl oz whipping cream

225 g/8 oz crunchy peanut butter

Pour the milk into a heavy-based saucepan, add the vanilla extract and bring almost to the boil. Remove from the heat. Put the egg yolks and sugar in a large bowl and whisk together until pale and the mixture leaves a trail when the whisk is lifted. Slowly add the milk to the sugar mixture, stirring all the time with a wooden spoon.

Strain the mixture into the rinsed-out saucepan or a double boiler and cook over a low heat for 10–15 minutes, stirring all the time, until the mixture thickens enough to coat the back of the wooden spoon. Do not allow the mixture to boil or it will curdle.

Remove the custard from the heat, add the peanut butter and stir together until the mixture is smooth. Leave to cool for at least 1 hour, stirring from time to time to prevent a skin from forming. Meanwhile, whip the cream until it holds its shape. Keep in the refrigerator until ready to use.

If using an ice cream machine, fold the whipped cream into the cold custard, then churn the mixture in the machine following the manufacturer's instructions. Alternatively, freeze the custard in a freezerproof container, uncovered, for 1–2 hours until beginning to set around the edges. Turn the custard into a bowl and stir with a fork or beat in a food processor until smooth. Fold in the whipped cream. Return to the freezer and freeze for a further 2–3 hours, or until firm or required. Cover the container with a lid for storing.

serves 6–8

300 ml/10 fl oz milk

100 g/3¹/₂ oz milk chocolate

3 egg yolks

85 g/3 oz caster sugar

300 ml/10 fl oz whipping cream

100 g/3¹/₂ oz plain chocolate

50 g/1³/₄ oz blanched almonds

50 g/1³/₄ oz white mini marshmallows

50 g/1³/₄ oz glacé cherries

rocky road ice cream

Pour the milk into a heavy-based saucepan. Break the milk chocolate into the milk and heat gently, stirring all the time, until melted and smooth. Remove from the heat. Put the egg yolks and sugar in a larger bowl and whisk together until pale and the mixture leaves a trail when the whisk is lifted. Slowly add the chocolate mixture, stirring all the time with a wooden spoon.

Strain the mixture into the rinsed-out saucepan or a double boiler and cook over a low heat for 10–15 minutes, stirring all the time, until the mixture thickens enough to coat the back of the wooden spoon. Do not allow the mixture to boil or it will curdle.

Remove the custard from the heat and leave to cool for at least 1 hour, stirring from time to time to prevent a skin from forming. Meanwhile, whip the cream until it holds its shape. Keep in the refrigerator until ready to use. Roughly chop the plain chocolate and almonds. Cut the marshmallows and cherries into quarters.

If using an ice cream machine, fold the whipped cream into the cold custard, then churn the mixture in the machine following the manufacturer's instructions. Just before the ice cream freezes, add the chopped chocolate, almonds, marshmallows and cherries. Alternatively, freeze the custard in a freezerproof container, uncovered, for 1–2 hours, or until it begins to set around the edges. Turn the custard into a bowl and stir with a fork or beat in a food processor until smooth. Fold in the whipped cream, chopped chocolate, almonds, marshmallows and cherries. Return to the freezer and freeze for a further 2–3 hours, or until firm or required. Cover the container with a lid for storing.

serves 6

125 g/4 oz amaretti biscuits

300 ml/10 fl oz double cream

150 ml/5 fl oz single cream

115 g/4 oz icing sugar

4 tbsp Marsala

biscuit tortoni

Line a 450-g/1-lb loaf tin or 850-ml/1½-pint oblong freezerproof plastic container with greaseproof paper, allowing it to hang over the edges of the container so that the ice cream can be easily removed. Put the biscuits in a food processor and process to form fine crumbs. Alternatively, put the biscuits in a strong polythene bag and crush with a rolling pin.

Pour the double cream and single cream into a large bowl and whip together until the mixture holds its shape. Sift the icing sugar into the whipped cream, then fold in with the Marsala. Fold in the biscuits, reserving a third.

Pour the mixture into the prepared tin, smooth the surface and freeze, uncovered, for 5 hours, or until firm or required. Cover the container with a lid for storing.

Take the ice cream out of the freezer about 30 minutes before you are ready to serve it. Uncover, turn out on to a serving dish and remove the greaseproof paper. Leave at room temperature to soften. Using a palette knife, press the reserved crushed biscuits lightly onto the top and sides of the ice cream until it is evenly coated. Serve cut into thick slices.

serves 4–6

300 ml/10 fl oz milk

3 egg yolks

85 g/3 oz soft light brown sugar

300 ml/10 fl oz whipping cream

55 g/2 oz stem ginger

1 tbsp stem ginger syrup

ginger ice cream

Pour the milk into a heavy-based saucepan and bring almost to the boil. Remove from the heat. Put the egg yolks and sugar in a large bowl and whisk together until pale and the mixture leaves a trail when the whisk is lifted. Slowly add the milk to the sugar mixture, stirring constantly with a wooden spoon.

Strain the mixture into the rinsed-out saucepan or a double boiler and cook over a low heat for 10–15 minutes, stirring constantly, until the mixture thickens enough to coat the back of the wooden spoon. Do not allow the mixture to boil or it will curdle.

Remove the custard from the heat and leave to cool for at least 1 hour, stirring from time to time to prevent a skin from forming. Meanwhile, whip the cream until it holds its shape. Keep in the refrigerator until ready to use. Finely chop the ginger. When the custard is cold, stir the ginger syrup into it.

If using an ice cream machine, fold the whipped cream into the cold custard, then churn the mixture in the machine following the manufacturer's instructions. Just before the ice cream freezes, add the chopped ginger. Alternatively, freeze the custard in a freezerproof container, uncovered, for 1–2 hours until beginning to set around the edges. Turn the custard into a bowl and stir with a fork or beat in a food processor until smooth. Fold in the whipped cream and chopped ginger. Return to the freezer and freeze for a further 2–3 hours until firm or until required. Cover the container with a lid for storing.

serves 4

150 ml/5 fl oz milk

600 ml/1 pint whipping cream

4 tbsp fresh coffee

3 large egg yolks

115 g/4 oz caster sugar

cocoa powder, for dusting

chocolate-coated coffee beans, to decorate

cappuccino ice cream

Pour the milk and 450 ml/16 fl oz of the cream into a heavy-based saucepan, stir in the coffee and bring almost to the boil. Remove from the heat, leave to infuse for 5 minutes, then strain through a filter paper or a sieve lined with muslin.

Put the egg yolks and sugar in a large bowl and whisk together until pale and creamy. Slowly add the milk mixture, stirring all the time with a wooden spoon. Strain the mixture into the rinsed-out saucepan or a double boiler and cook over a low heat for 10–15 minutes, stirring all the time, until the mixture thickens enough to coat the back of the spoon. Do not allow the mixture to boil or it will curdle. Remove the custard from the heat and leave to cool for at least 1 hour, stirring from time to time to prevent a skin from forming.

If using an ice cream machine, churn the cold custard in the machine following the manufacturer's instructions. Alternatively, freeze the custard in a freezerproof container, uncovered, for 1–2 hours, or until it begins to set around the edges. Turn the custard into a bowl and stir with a fork or beat in a food processor until smooth. Return to the freezer and freeze for a further 2–3 hours, or until firm or required. Cover the container with a lid for storing.

champagne sorbet

serves 6

225 g/8 oz caster sugar

300 ml/10 fl oz water

1/2 bottle pink or white champagne or sparkling wine

juice of 1/2 lemon

1 egg white

Put the sugar and water in a heavy-based saucepan and heat gently, stirring, until the sugar has dissolved. Bring to the boil, then cook, without stirring, over a medium heat for 2 minutes.

Remove the syrup from the heat and leave to cool for at least 1 hour. When cold, stir the champagne and lemon juice into the syrup.

If using an ice cream machine, churn the mixture in the machine following the manufacturer's instructions. When the mixture begins to freeze, whisk the egg white until it just holds its shape but is not dry, then add to the mixture and continue churning. Alternatively, freeze the custard in a freezerproof container, uncovered, for 3 hours, or until mushy. Turn the mixture into a bowl and stir with a fork or beat in a food processor to break down the ice crystals. Lightly whisk the egg white until stiff but not dry, then fold it into the mixture. Return the sorbet to the freezer and freeze for a further 3–4 hours, or until firm or required. Cover the container with a lid for storing.

3

Fruity Freezes

serves 6–8

300 ml/10 fl oz milk

1 vanilla pod

210 g/7½ oz caster sugar

3 egg yolks

350 g/12 oz fresh raspberries

6 tbsp water

300 ml/10 fl oz whipping cream

raspberry ripple ice cream

Pour the milk into a heavy-based saucepan, add the vanilla pod and bring almost to the boil. Remove from the heat and leave to infuse for 30 minutes. Put 85 g/3 oz of the sugar and the egg yolks in a large bowl and whisk together until pale and the mixture leaves a trail when the whisk is lifted. Remove the vanilla pod from the milk, then slowly add the milk to the sugar mixture, stirring all the time with a wooden spoon.

Strain the mixture into the rinsed-out saucepan or a double boiler and cook over a low heat for 10–15 minutes, stirring all the time, until the mixture thickens enough to coat the back of the wooden spoon. Do not allow the mixture to boil or it will curdle. Remove the custard from the heat and leave to cool for at least 1 hour, stirring from time to time to prevent a skin from forming.

Meanwhile, put the raspberries in a heavy-based saucepan with the remaining 125 g/4½ oz of sugar and the water. Heat gently, stirring, until the sugar has dissolved, then simmer gently for 5 minutes, or until the raspberries are very soft. Pass the raspberries through a nylon sieve into a bowl to remove the seeds, then leave the purée to cool. Meanwhile, whip the cream until it holds its shape. Keep in the refrigerator until ready to use.

If using an ice cream machine, fold the whipped cream into the cold custard, then churn the mixture in the machine following the manufacturer's instructions. Just before the ice cream freezes, spread half into a freezerproof container. Pour over half the raspberry purée then repeat the layers. Freeze for 1–2 hours or until firm or required.

serves 6

115 g/4 oz caster sugar

150 ml/5 fl oz water

225 g/8 oz fresh cherries, stoned, plus extra whole cherries to decorate

2 tbsp freshly squeezed orange juice

300 ml/10 fl oz double cream

150 ml/5 fl oz single cream

crushed cherry ice cream

Put the sugar and water in a heavy-based saucepan and heat gently, stirring, until the sugar has dissolved, then bring to the boil and boil for 3 minutes. Reduce the heat, add the cherries and simmer gently for about 10 minutes, or until soft. Leave the mixture to cool for at least 1 hour.

When the cherries are cold, put them in a food processor or blender with the syrup. Add the orange juice and process the cherries until just roughly chopped. Do not blend too much as the cherries should be crushed, not puréed. Pour the double and single cream into a large bowl and whip together until the mixture holds its shape. Fold in the crushed cherries.

If using an ice cream machine, churn the mixture in the machine following the manufacturer's instructions. Alternatively, freeze the mixture in a freezerproof container, uncovered, for 1–2 hours, or until it begins to set around the edges. Turn the mixture into a bowl and stir with a fork or beat in a food processor until smooth. Return to the freezer and freeze for a further 2–3 hours, or until firm or required. Cover the container with a lid for storing. Serve decorated with whole cherries.

serves 6

600 ml/1 pint coconut milk

175 g/6 oz caster sugar

6 egg yolks

175 g/6 oz desiccated coconut

150 ml/5 fl oz double cream

1 tbsp Malibu (optional)

tropical fruits

2 pawpaws, peeled, deseeded and thinly sliced

2 star fruit, thinly sliced

2 kiwi fruit, peeled and thinly sliced

1 tbsp caster sugar

coconut ice cream with tropical fruits

Pour the coconut milk into a saucepan and heat gently. Remove from the heat. Put the sugar and egg yolks in a large bowl and whisk together until pale and the mixture leaves a trail when the whisk is lifted. Slowly add the coconut milk, stirring all the time with a wooden spoon. Strain the mixture into the rinsed-out saucepan or a double boiler and cook over a low heat for 10–15 minutes, stirring all the time, until the mixture thickens enough to coat the back of the spoon. If the mixture separates, simply whisk it vigorously until it is smooth again. Do not allow the mixture to boil or it will curdle.

Remove the custard from the heat, stir in the desiccated coconut, then leave to cool for at least 1 hour, stirring from time to time to prevent a skin from forming. Meanwhile, whip the cream until it just holds its shape. Keep in the refrigerator until ready to use. When the custard is cold, add the Malibu, if using, and mix well together.

If using an ice cream machine, fold the cold custard into the whipped cream, then churn the mixture in the machine following the manufacturer's instructions. Alternatively, freeze the custard in a freezerproof container, uncovered, for 1–2 hours, or until it begins to set around the edges. Turn the custard into a bowl and stir with a fork or beat in a food processor until smooth. Fold in the whipped cream. Return to the freezer and freeze for a further 2–3 hours, or until firm or required. Cover the container with a lid for storing.

Place the fruits in a large shallow dish. Sprinkle the sugar over the fruit, then cover and chill in the refrigerator for 2–3 hours before serving with the ice cream.

lime & mascarpone ice cream

serves 4–6

125 ml/4 fl oz bottled lime juice or cordial

500 g/1 lb 2 oz mascarpone cheese

175 g/6 oz icing sugar

150 ml/5 fl oz whipping cream

Put the lime juice in a bowl, add the mascarpone and beat together. Sift the icing sugar into the mixture and beat again until well blended. Whip the cream until it holds its shape. Keep in the refrigerator until ready to use.

If using an ice cream machine, fold the whipped cream into the mascarpone mixture, then churn in the machine following the manufacturer's instructions. Alternatively, freeze the mixture in a freezerproof container, uncovered, for 1–2 hours, or until it begins to set around the edges. Turn the mixture into a bowl and stir with a fork or beat in a food processor until smooth. Fold in the whipped cream. Return to the freezer and freeze for a further 2–3 hours, or until firm or required. Cover the container with a lid for storing.

banana ice cream

serves 8

3 bananas

2 tbsp lemon juice

1 tbsp white rum (optional)

115 g/4 oz icing sugar

600 ml/1 pint whipping cream

Peel and slice the bananas, then put the flesh in a food processor or blender. Add the lemon juice and process to form a very smooth purée. Turn the mixture into a large bowl. Alternatively, sprinkle the lemon juice over the banana slices, then push the flesh through a nylon sieve to form a purée. Add the rum, if using, and mix well together.

Sift the icing sugar into the mixture and beat until well mixed. Whip the cream until it holds its shape. Keep in the refrigerator until ready to use.

If using an ice cream machine, fold the whipped cream into the banana mixture, then churn the mixture in the machine following the manufacturer's instructions. Alternatively, freeze the mixture in a freezerproof container, uncovered, for 1–2 hours, or until it begins to set around the edges. Turn the mixture into a bowl and stir with a fork or beat in a food processor until smooth. Fold in the whipped cream. Return to the freezer and freeze for a further 2–3 hours, or until firm or required. Cover the container with a lid for storing.

serves 4–6

6 tbsp lemon juice

500 ml/18 fl oz Greek yogurt

150 ml/5 fl oz for double cream

100 g/3^1/$_2$ oz caster sugar

ice bowl

2 lemons

mint or lemon-scented geranium leaves (optional)

water

lemon yogurt ice cream in an ice bowl

To make the ice bowl, thinly slice the lemons and discard the pips. Use the lemon slices and mint leaves, if using, to line the base and sides of a 1^1/$_2$-litre/2^3/$_4$-pint freezerproof bowl. Insert a 1-litre/1^3/$_4$-pint freezerproof bowl inside and fill the space between the two bowls with water. Immediately place a plate and heavy weight on top. Carefully transfer the bowl to the freezer and freeze for at least 4 hours, until frozen.

Meanwhile, to make the ice cream, put the lemon juice into a bowl, add the yogurt, cream and caster sugar and mix well together.

If using an ice cream machine, churn the mixture in the machine following the manufacturer's instructions. Alternatively, freeze the mixture in a freezerproof container, uncovered, for 1–2 hours, or until beginning to set around the edges. Turn the mixture into a bowl and stir with a fork or beat in a food processor until smooth. Return to the freezer and freeze for a further 2–3 hours, or until firm or required. Cover the container with a lid for storing.

To use the ice bowl, remove the weight and plate and quickly run the bowls under hot water until they loosen, then remove the ice bowl. Quickly transfer the ice bowl to a serving plate and return to the freezer until ready to use.

About 30 minutes before serving the ice cream, remove it from the freezer and leave at room temperature to allow it to soften slightly. Spoon into the ice bowl and serve.

pear ice cream

serves 4–6

400 g/14 oz canned pear halves in fruit juice, drained

300 ml/10 fl oz milk

3 egg yolks

85 g/3 oz soft light brown sugar

300 ml/10 fl oz whipping cream

Put the pear halves in a food processor and blend until smooth. Pour the milk into a heavy-based saucepan and bring almost to the boil. Remove from the heat.

Put the egg yolks and sugar in a large bowl and whisk together until pale and the mixture leaves a trail when the whisk is lifted. Slowly add the milk, stirring all the time with a wooden spoon.

Strain the mixture into the rinsed-out saucepan or a double boiler and cook over a low heat for 10–15 minutes, stirring all the time, until the mixture thickens enough to coat the back of the wooden spoon. Do not allow the mixture to boil or it will curdle.

Remove the custard from the heat and stir in the pear purée. Leave to cool for at least 1 hour, stirring from time to time to prevent a skin from forming. Meanwhile, whip the cream until it holds its shape. Keep in the refrigerator until ready to use.

If using an ice cream machine, fold the whipped cream into the cold custard, then churn the mixture in the machine following the manufacturer's instructions. Alternatively, freeze the custard in a freezerproof container, uncovered, for 1–2 hours until beginning to set around the edges. Turn the custard into a bowl and stir with a fork or beat in a food processor until smooth. Fold in the whipped cream. Return to the freezer and freeze for a further 2–3 hours, or until firm or required. Cover the container with a lid for storing.

serves 4–6

125 g/4$^{1}/_{2}$ oz blueberries

300 ml/10 fl oz Greek yogurt

300 ml/10 fl oz double cream

85 g/3 oz caster sugar

1 tsp vanilla extract

juice of 1 lemon

blueberry ice cream

Put the blueberries in a food processor and blend together until roughly chopped. Transfer to a large bowl.

Add the yogurt, cream, caster sugar, vanilla extract and lemon juice to the blueberries and mix well together.

If using an ice cream machine, churn the mixture in the machine following the manufacturer's instructions. Alternatively, freeze the mixture in a freezerproof container, uncovered, for 1–2 hours, or until beginning to set around the edges. Turn the mixture into a bowl and stir with a fork or beat in a food processor until smooth. Return to the freezer and freeze for a further 2–3 hours, or until firm or required. Cover the container with a lid for storing.

orange ice cream

serves 6–8

300 ml/10 fl oz milk

85 g/3 oz caster sugar

3 egg yolks

300 ml/10 fl oz double cream

3 large oranges, plus 3 extra oranges, segmented, to serve

Pour the milk into a saucepan and bring almost to the boil. Remove from the heat. Put the sugar and egg yolks in a large bowl and whisk together until pale and the mixture leaves a trail when the whisk is lifted. Slowly add the milk, stirring all the time with a wooden spoon. Strain the mixture into the rinsed-out saucepan or a double boiler and cook over a low heat for 10–15 minutes, stirring all the time, until the mixture thickens enough to coat the back of the spoon. Do not allow the mixture to boil or it will curdle. Remove the custard from the heat and leave to cool for at least 1 hour, stirring from time to time to prevent a skin from forming.

Meanwhile, finely grate the rind from 1 of the oranges and squeeze the juice from all 3 oranges – you should have about 350 ml/12 fl oz of juice in total. If wished, reserve the orange skins for serving. Whip the cream until it just holds its shape. Keep in the refrigerator until ready to use. When the custard is cold, add the orange rind and juice and mix well together.

If using an ice cream machine, fold the cold custard into the whipped cream, then churn the mixture in the machine following the manufacturer's instructions. Alternatively, freeze the custard in a freezerproof container, uncovered, for 1–2 hours, or until it begins to set around the edges. Turn the custard into a bowl and stir with a fork or beat in a food processor until smooth. Fold in the whipped cream. Return to the freezer and freeze for a further 2–3 hours, or until firm or required. Cover the container with a lid for storing. Serve with the orange segments.

serves 6

175 g/6 oz caster sugar

425 ml/15 fl oz water

6–9 large lemons

lemon slices, to decorate

lemon water ice

Put the sugar and water in a heavy-based saucepan and heat gently, stirring, until the sugar has dissolved. Bring to the boil, then boil, without stirring, for 10 minutes to form a syrup. Do not allow it to brown.

Meanwhile, using a potato peeler, thinly pare the rind from 4 of the lemons. Remove the syrup from the heat and add the pared lemon rind. Leave to cool for at least 1 hour.

Squeeze the juice from the lemons and strain into a measuring jug – you need 425 ml/15 fl oz in total. When the syrup is cold, strain it into a bowl, add the lemon juice and stir together until well mixed.

If using an ice cream machine, churn the mixture in the machine following the manufacturer's instructions. Alternatively, freeze the mixture in a freezerproof container, uncovered, for 3–4 hours, or until mushy. Turn the mixture into a bowl and stir with a fork or beat in a food processor to break down the ice crystals. Return to the freezer and freeze for a further 3–4 hours, or until firm or required. Cover the container with a lid for storing. Serve decorated with lemon slices.

serves 4–6

2 large ripe mangoes

juice of 1 lemon

pinch of salt

115 g/4 oz caster sugar

3 tbsp water

mango sorbet

Using a sharp knife, thinly peel the mangoes, holding them over a bowl to catch the juices. Cut the flesh away from the central stone and put in a food processor or blender. Add the mango juice, lemon juice and salt and process to form a smooth purée. Push the mango purée through a nylon sieve into the bowl.

Put the sugar and water in a heavy-based saucepan and heat gently, stirring, until the sugar has dissolved. Bring to the boil, without stirring, then remove from the heat and leave to cool slightly.

Pour the syrup into the mango purée and mix well together. Leave to cool, then chill the mango syrup in the refrigerator for 2 hours, or until cold.

If using an ice cream machine, churn the mixture in the machine following the manufacturer's instructions. Alternatively, freeze the mixture in a freezerproof container, uncovered, for 3–4 hours, or until mushy. Turn the mixture into a bowl and stir with a fork or beat in a food processor to break down the ice crystals. Return to the freezer and freeze for a further 3–4 hours, or until firm or required. Cover the container with a lid for storing.

serves 6

225 g/8 oz redcurrants, plus extra to decorate

225 g/8 oz raspberries, plus extra to decorate

175 ml/6 fl oz water

115 g/4 oz caster sugar

150 ml/5 fl oz cranberry juice

2 egg whites

red berry sorbet

Strip the redcurrants from their stalks using the prongs of a fork and put them in a large heavy-based saucepan together with the raspberries. Add 30 ml/1 fl oz of the water and cook over a medium heat for 10 minutes, or until soft. Push the fruit through a nylon sieve into a bowl to form a purée.

Put the sugar and the remaining water into the rinsed-out saucepan and heat gently, stirring, until the sugar has dissolved. Bring to the boil, then boil, without stirring, for 10 minutes to form a syrup. Do not allow it to brown. Remove from the heat and leave to cool for at least 1 hour. When cold, stir the fruit purée and cranberry juice into the syrup.

If using an ice cream machine, churn the mixture in the machine following the manufacturer's instructions. When the mixture begins to freeze, whisk the egg whites until they just hold their shape but are not dry, then add to the mixture and continue churning. Alternatively, freeze the mixture in a freezerproof container, uncovered, for 3–4 hours, or until mushy. Turn the mixture into a bowl and stir with a fork or beat in a food processor to break down the ice crystals. Lightly whisk the egg whites until stiff but not dry, then fold them into the mixture. Return to the freezer and freeze for a further 3–4 hours, or until firm or required. Cover the container with a lid for storing. Serve scattered with extra fruits.

4

Something
Saucy

chocolate sauce

serves 4–6

300 ml/10 fl oz milk

25 g/1 oz butter

85 g/3 oz caster sugar

85 g/3 oz soft light brown soft sugar

85 g/3 oz cocoa powder

Put all the ingredients in a heavy-based saucepan. Heat gently, stirring all the time, until the sugar has dissolved, then bring to the boil and boil, without stirring, for 2 minutes, or until the sauce coats the back of a wooden spoon.

Serve the sauce poured over ice cream of your choice.

serves 4–6

125 g/4^1/$_2$ oz caster sugar

125 ml/4 fl oz water

1 tbsp lemon juice

150 ml/5 fl oz single cream

caramel sauce

Put the sugar, water and lemon juice in a heavy-based saucepan. Heat gently, stirring all the time, until the sugar has dissolved, then bring to the boil and boil, without stirring, for 5 minutes, or until the mixture turns a pale caramel colour.

Remove the sauce from the heat and gradually stir in the cream. Leave to cool, then chill in the refrigerator for at least 3 hours. Serve the sauce poured over ice cream of your choice.

butterscotch sauce

serves 6

55 g/2 oz butter

140 g/5 oz soft light brown sugar

140 g/5 oz golden syrup

150 ml/5 fl oz double cream

Put the butter, sugar and syrup in a heavy-based saucepan. Heat gently, stirring all the time, until the butter has melted and the sugar has dissolved, then simmer gently, stirring occasionally, for about 5 minutes, or until a thick sauce has formed.

Remove the sauce from the heat and gradually stir in the cream. Serve the sauce hot or cold, poured over ice cream of your choice.

serves 6

350 g/12 oz fresh or frozen
raspberries

1 tsp lemon juice

2 tbsp icing sugar

2 tbsp framboise liqueur
(optional)

raspberry sauce

If using frozen raspberries, allow to thaw at room temperature
for 3–4 hours. Put the raspberries and lemon juice in a food
processor or blender and blend to form a smooth purée. Push
through a nylon sieve into a bowl to remove the seeds.

Sift the sugar into the raspberries and stir together. If using, stir
in the liqueur. Chill in the refrigerator for at least 1 hour before
serving. Serve the sauce poured over ice cream of your choice.

hot chocolate fudge sauce

serves 4–6

50 g/1³/4 oz plain chocolate

25 g/1 oz butter

4 tbsp milk

225 g/8 oz soft light brown sugar

2 tbsp golden syrup

The sauce should be served hot so make it just before you are going to serve the ice cream. Stand a bowl over a saucepan of simmering water. Break the chocolate into the bowl and add the butter and milk. Heat gently, stirring occasionally, until the chocolate has melted and the sauce is smooth.

Transfer the mixture to a heavy-based saucepan and stir in the sugar and syrup. Heat gently, stirring all the time, until the sugar has dissolved, then bring to the boil and boil, without stirring, for 5 minutes. Serve the sauce hot, poured over ice cream of your choice.

cranberry & orange sauce

serves 4–6

225 g/8 oz fresh or frozen cranberries

300 ml/10 fl oz fresh orange juice

1 cinnamon stick

100 g/3½ oz caster sugar

juice of ½ lemon

Put the cranberries, orange juice and cinnamon stick in a heavy-based saucepan. Bring to the boil, then reduce the heat and simmer, uncovered, for 15–20 minutes, or until the cranberries have burst. Leave to cool slightly then remove the cinnamon stick.

Pour the cranberries into a food processor or blender and blend to form a smooth purée. Push through a nylon sieve into a bowl to remove the seeds.

Return the cranberries to the rinsed-out saucepan and add the sugar. Heat gently, stirring all the time, until the sugar has dissolved. Stir in the lemon juice. Leave the sauce to cool, then chill in the refrigerator for at least 3 hours. Serve the sauce poured over ice cream of your choice.

apricot & brandy sauce

serves 6–8

225 g/8 oz dried apricots

3 tbsp brandy

300 ml/10 fl oz fresh orange juice

Put the apricots in a bowl and add the brandy. Leave to soak for 3–4 hours, stirring occasionally, until the liquid is absorbed.

Put the soaked apricots in a food processor or blender and add the orange juice. Blend to form a smooth purée. Serve the sauce poured over ice cream of your choice.